On Our Street

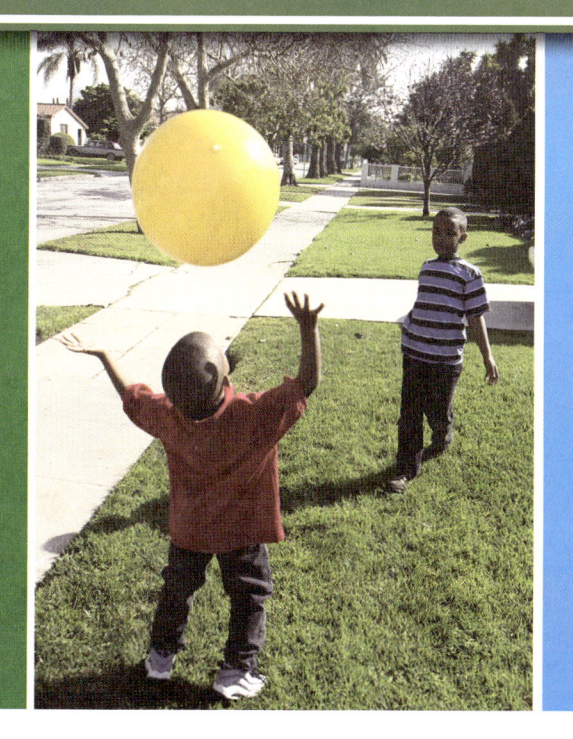

by Mathilda Prince

PEARSON

Glenview, Illinois • Boston, Massachusetts
Chandler, Arizona • Upper Saddle River, New Jersey

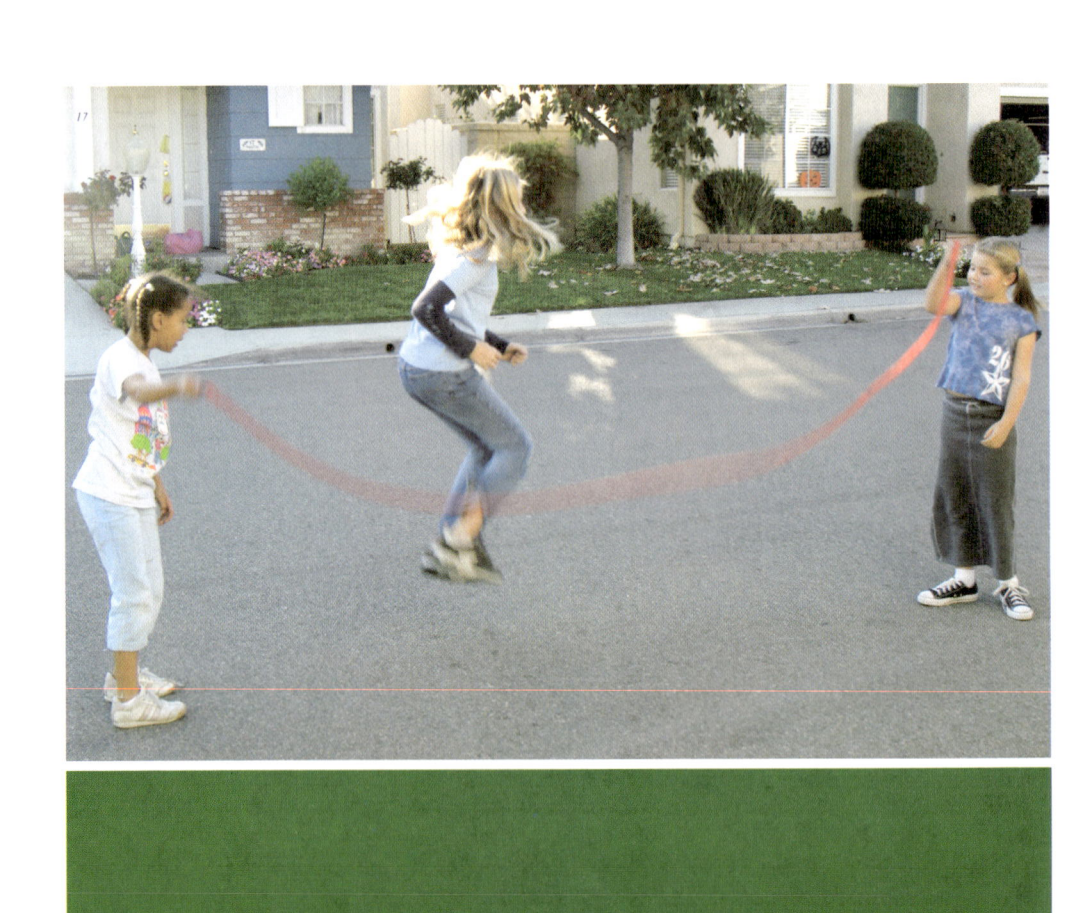

We jump.

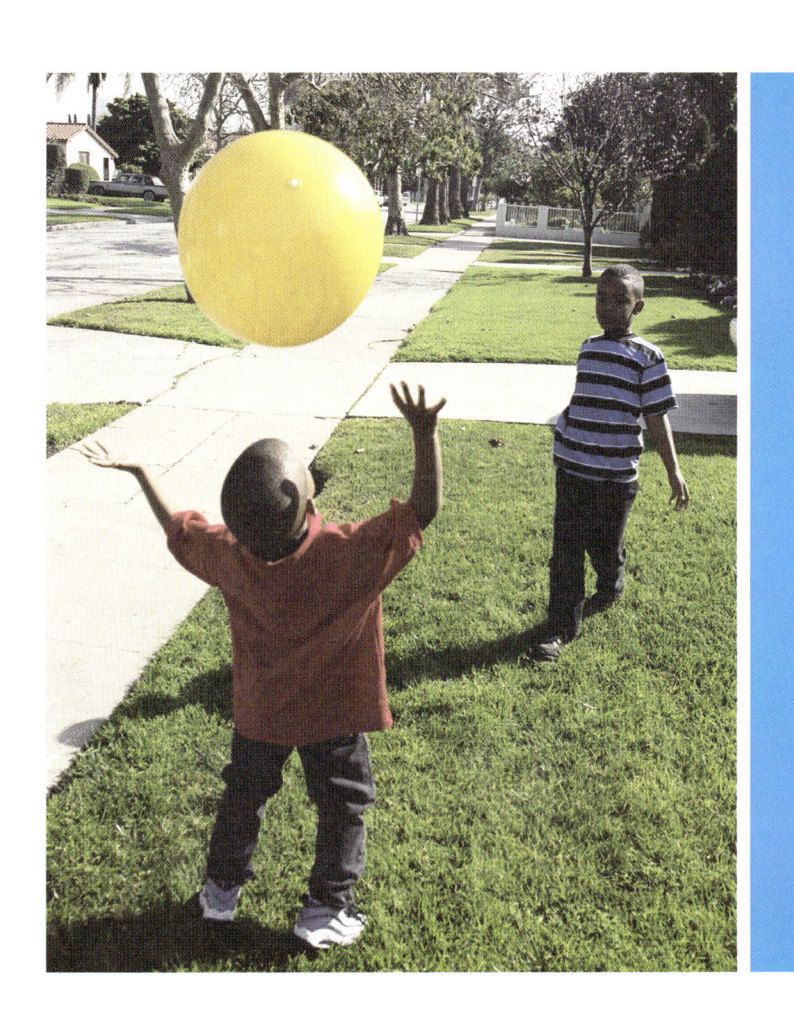

We play.

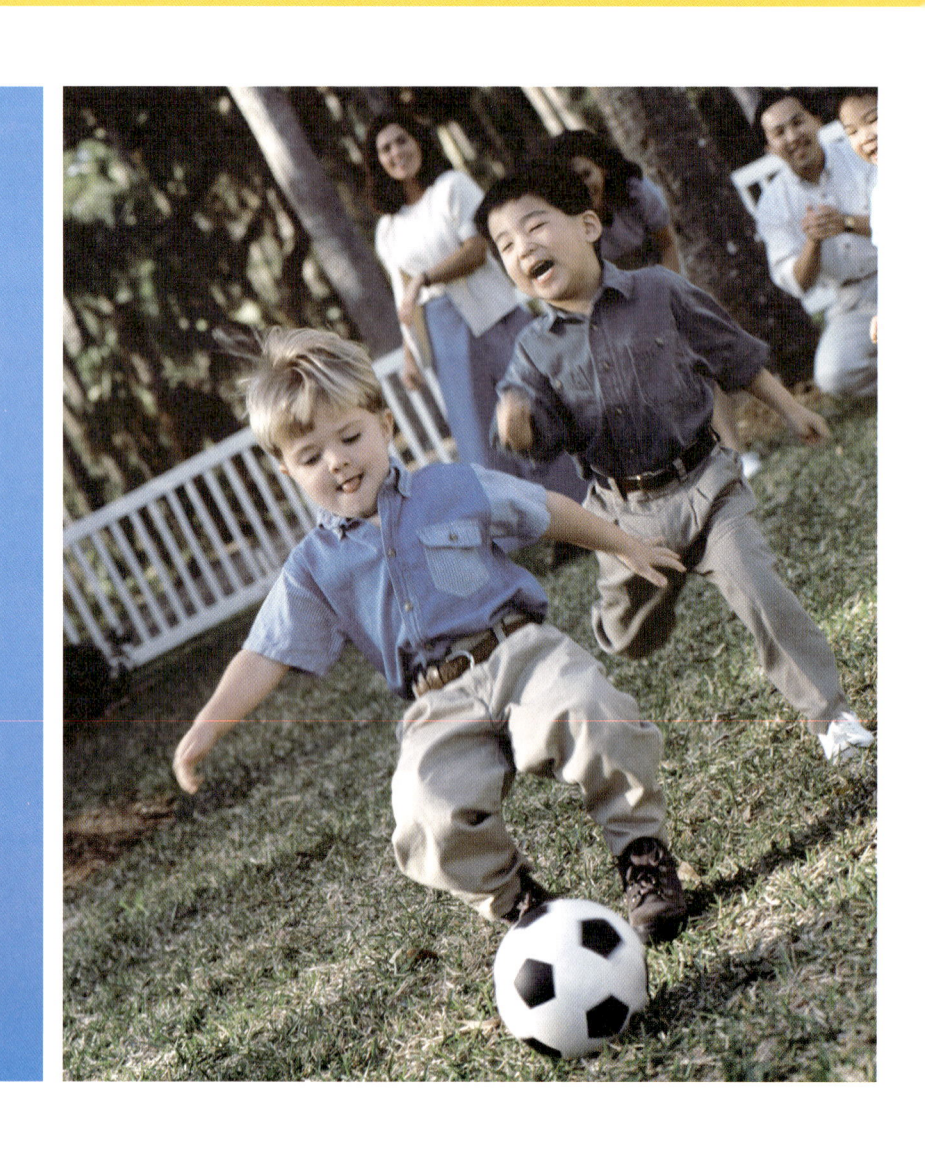

We run.

4

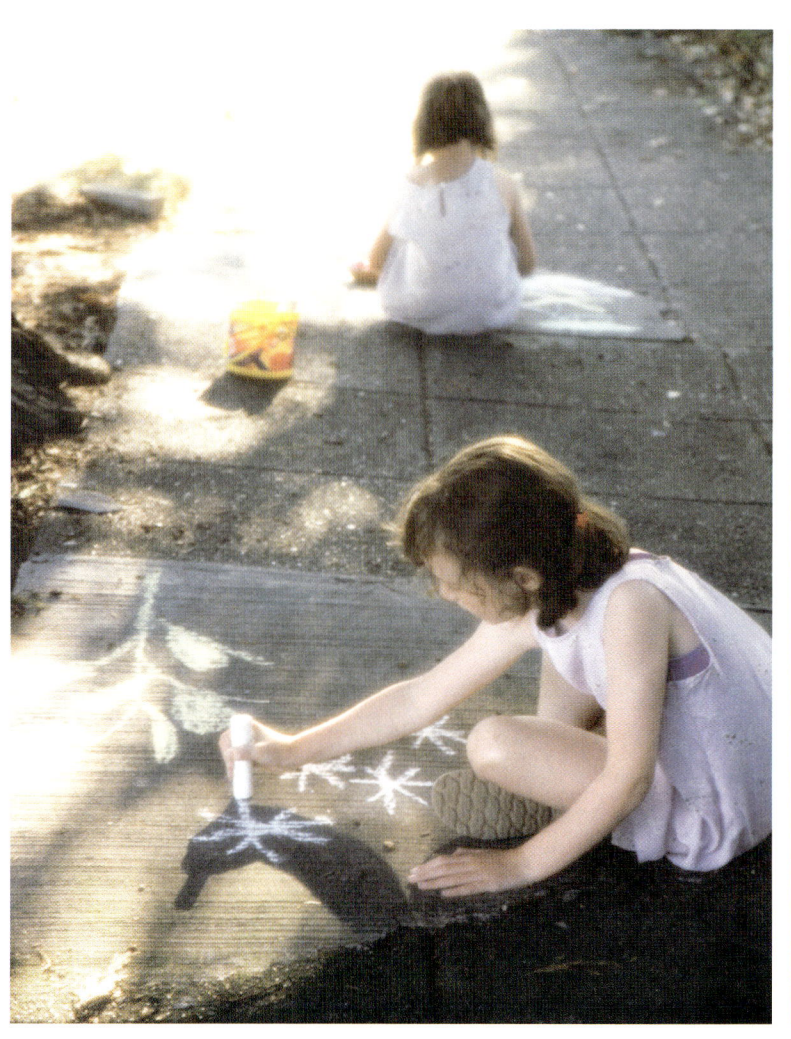

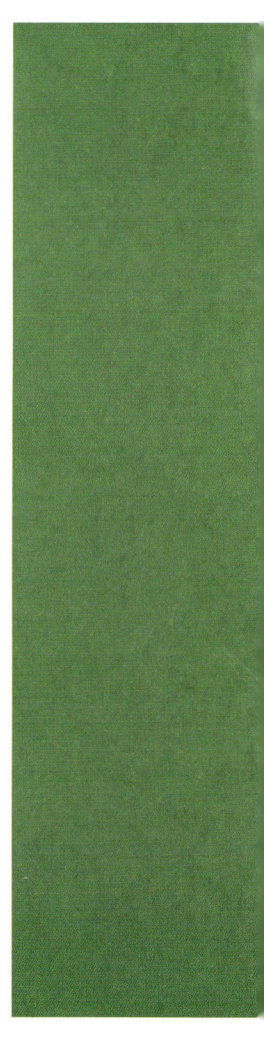

It is fun!

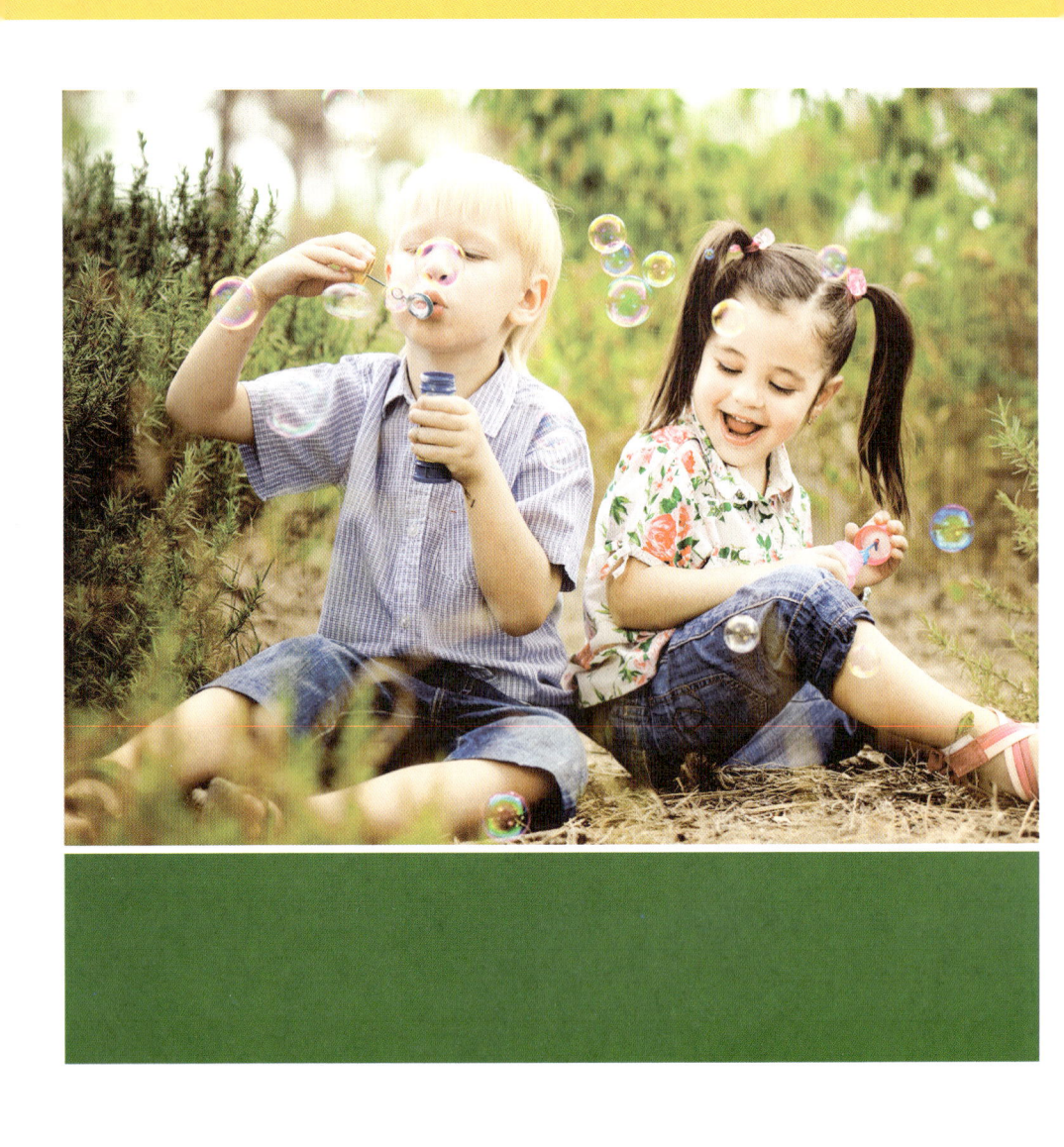

Pop! Pop! Pop!

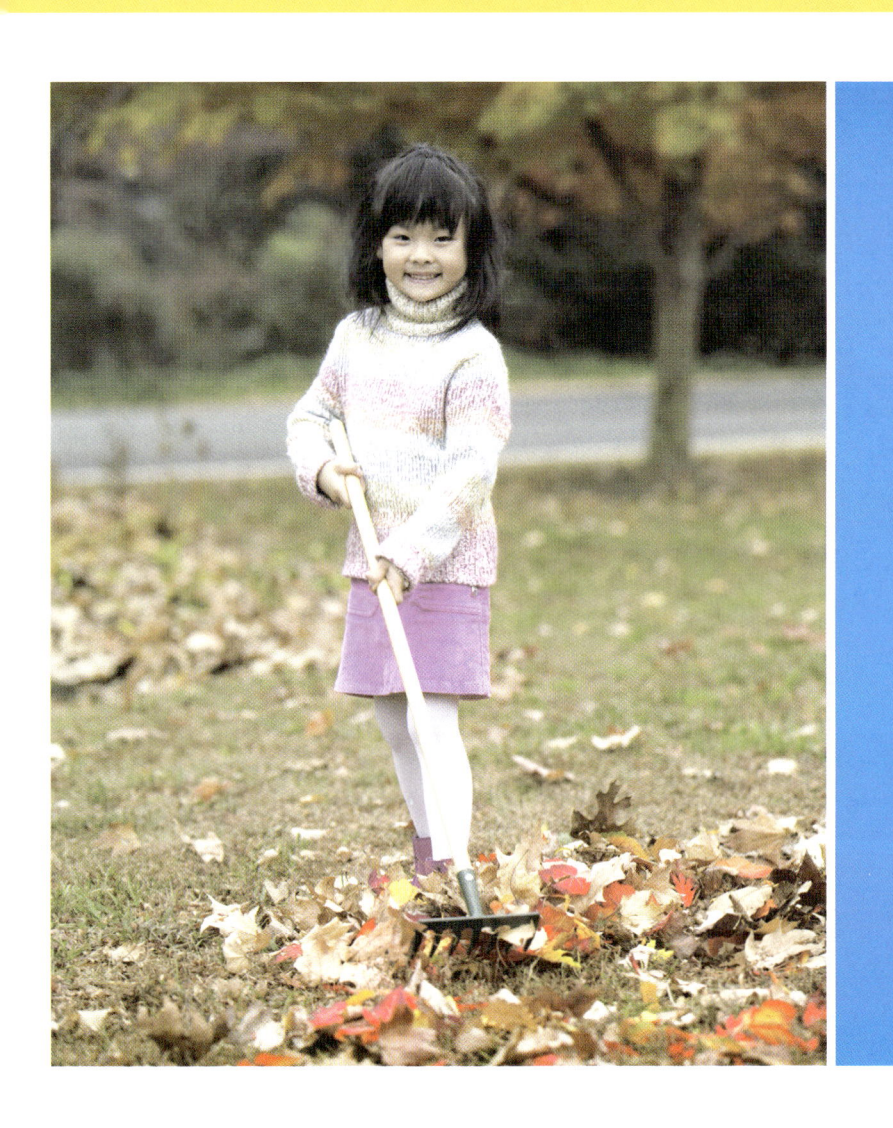

We help.

7

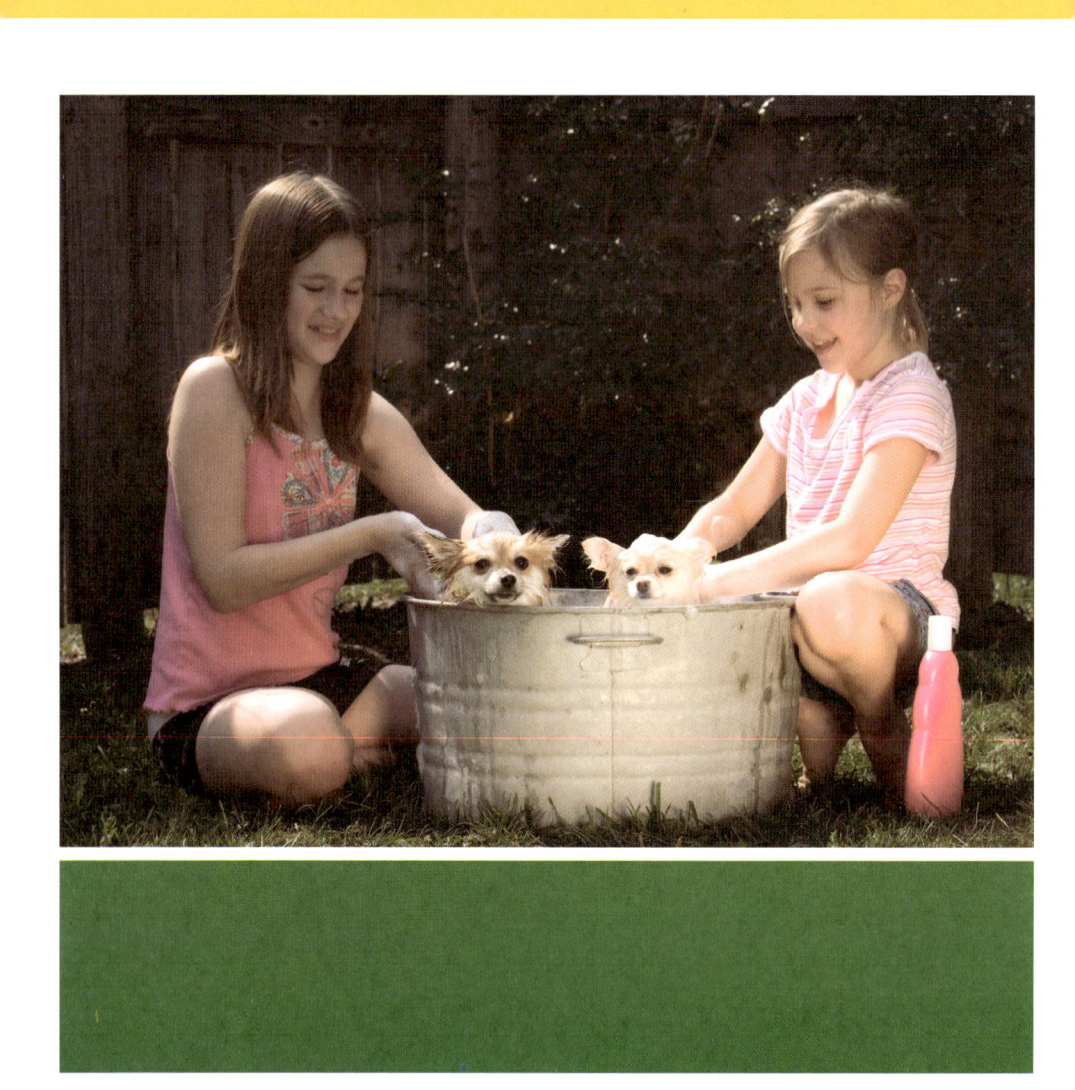

We help here.
We play here.